Catching Vision

Seeing a New Future for Your Church

Participant's Guide

Terry Tieman

TCN
TRANSFORMING
CHURCHES
NETWORK

For more information, please contact
Transforming Churches Network
1160 Vickery Ln. Ste #1, Cordova, TN 38016
901-757-9700
www.tcnprocess.com
terry@transformingchurchesnetwork.org

Table of Contents

Introduction

You have saved up your money, coordinated your vacation days with the kids' school break, studied all the brochures, bought the tickets, and reserved hotel rooms. Now you and your family are off to Disney World. This trip did not just appear on the horizon like today's weather; it was the greatly anticipated culmination of plans and activities that led up to this day. Because it will be expensive, requiring some sacrifices on the part of each member of the family, you won't be able to afford the very best hotel or get to see every attraction. There will be differences of opinions as to which attractions to visit, and some compromise and concessions will be required. All in all, however, it will be worth all the effort.

Before any plans were laid out for this great experience, there was a vision: we are going to Disney World! This was a vision the entire family could get behind. Dad could see himself behind the camera as the kids engaged people in Disney costumes. Jenny could see herself going 'round and 'round in giant revolving tea cups, while Bret was setting his sights on more dignified pursuits at Epcot. Mom was setting aside funds for some break-away time from the souvenir stands to do some more serious shopping. The details of the hoped-for experience were diverse, but the vision was clear.

Churches also have visions of where they are going. And like the Orlando-bound family, the trip should be exciting and have goals for the greater good of all who are involved. Likewise there will be careful planning and expense involved; there will be details to agree upon; some compromise and alignment of values will be needed in order to get to a wonderfully anticipated destination.

In this study, we will talk about the essential character of vision for a congregation, the importance of having a stated vision, and the process involved in composing a vision statement.

Vision Changes Everything

Objective: *In order for a church to work together, there must be a clear common focus. This study will demonstrate how vision clarity launches churches into new life.*

Discovery Activity

Target Practice

Debrief

Question #1: Were you more successful at hitting the page with the big dot or the page with the small dot?

Question #2: How does having a sharp and clear focus impact results?

Learning Activity

The Starting Point of Vision

The words of Nehemiah son of Hakaliah: In the month of Kislev in the twentieth year, while I was in the citadel of Susa, Hanani, one of my brothers, came from Judah with some other men, and I questioned them about the Jewish remnant that had survived the exile, and also about Jerusalem. They said to me, "Those who survived the exile and are back in the province are in great trouble and disgrace. The wall of Jerusalem is broken down, and its gates have been burned with fire." When I heard these things, I sat down and wept. For some days I mourned and fasted and prayed before the God of heaven. —Nehemiah 1:1-4

Most of the time, we walk through life focusing our lives in a general direction—like the large dot—but we lack a focused vision. We do the right things. We go to church. We live moral lives. We are moving in the right general direction, but we don't have a clear sense of God's vision for our lives and for our churches.

When we see God's vision we move from the general to the specific. We see this in the life of Nehemiah. He was doing the right thing as a servant of the king. He was a good employee and a model citizen. But the story recounted in the book of Nehemiah tells us how God gave him a new vision and how this vision made a difference in Israel.

This focused vision was sparked when Nehemiah heard about the troubling experiences of those in his homeland of Judah. As he listened to the report about the state of Jerusalem, the reality of the situation grabbed his soul. He wept. He was troubled to the point of not being able to function according to normal patterns. This was not just a concern that affected his logical analysis of the situation. He was stirred to the core of his being.

While the book of Nehemiah recounts the actions that resulted from clear, focused vision, the story does not begin with the vision itself. God's visions don't begin in boardrooms, planning meetings, or strategy sessions. God's visions begin when we see reality and allow the Spirit of God to stir us to the point that we must cry out to him to do something about it.

His concern deepened into anxiety. The anxiety shifted to a burden. The burden morphed into brokenness before God. And the brokenness burst forth into a consuming passion.

This was much more than a passing notion that something must be done, although such can lead to some good ideas. Nehemiah found his mind becoming more and more engulfed by the situation. It changed his actions. It changed the way he appeared to others.

Little did he know that this stirring in his soul was the birthing of a vision. It was the start of a process of honing in on the focus that God would have for his life. And this is the way God's visions are birthed today.

Discussion Questions
• What impresses you about the strength of Nehemiah's emotional reaction as he heard about the state of his people?

• How did this give rise to a vision?

• Why do you think a deep passion that develops over a specific concern is so important for getting focused on God's vision?

Vision and the Church

Andy Stanley writes in his book *Visioneering*:

"What is a vision? Where do they come from? Visions are born in the soul of a man or woman who is consumed with the tension between what is and what could be. Anyone who is emotionally involved—frustrated, brokenhearted, maybe even angry—about the way things are in light of the way they believe things could be is a candidate for a vision. Visions form in the hearts of those who are dissatisfied with the status quo… Vision carries with it a sense of conviction. Anyone with a vision will tell you this is not merely something that could be done. This is something that should be done."[1]

Most churches, like most people, think of vision in a general way—doing good things, carrying out good activities, fulfilling the general mandates of the Bible. They see the big biblical principles or purposes of the church and try to move in that direction. For instance, the general principle of Jesus' vision "to seek and to save those who are lost" (Luke 19:10) serves as a general mandate for all of God's people. The church is called to carry out the Great Commission and "make disciples of all nations" and to love God and others as outlined in the Great Commandment. But these do not give specific direction to specific congregations for God's vision.

Great Commandment— Matthew 22:37-40
Great Commission—Matthew 28:19-20

God's vision for a local congregation fits within the parameters of the Great Commission and the Great Commandment, but it will always be more focused, honed in, and specific. Think of it this way: The general direction provided by the Great Commission and the Great Commandment are like the big dot from the opening exercise. The specific vision is like the small one.

The big dot general direction can come through logical planning and biblical application. Many different plans, programs, and initiatives seem good when we think in general terms, but when God clarifies his vision within the souls of his people, it provides razor-sharp focus for what needs to be done.

In the book *Leadership Challenge*, it states, "Visions are like lenses. They focus unrefracted rays of light. They enable everyone concerned with an enterprise to see more clearly what is ahead of them." This vision is key to the birthing of God's new ventures, along with the growth and maturity of them. If we were to graph how focused vision generates upward movement, it might look like this.

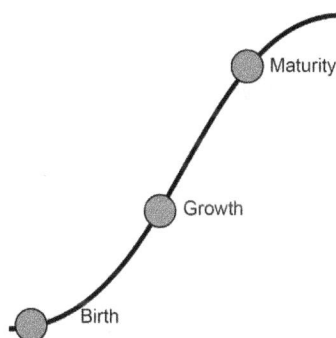

New vision births new ventures. And usually these visions are initiated in ways that are similar to the experience of Nehemiah. Something happens within the souls of God's people, and they begin to see that something needs to be done. Usually the process begins when God grabs the heart of a key leader or leaders and opens their eyes to a need that bothers them at the gut level. The need generates a concern. The concern deepens into anxiety. The anxiety shifts to a burden. The burden morphs into brokenness before God. And the brokenness breaks out into a consuming passion.

For Nehemiah, the vision began as he listened and as he sought to understand the dire needs of the situation. If he had never seen the need, he would have never been troubled to the point of passionate prayer. For the church today, it is much the same. We have to look outside into the world and see the need, allowing that to stir us to the point that we can go to God and receive his direction.

Discussion Questions
• How is a specific vision different from a general biblical direction?

• How does the story of Nehemiah provide an example of how vision for our church can begin?

• Why is seeing the needs and seeking to understand them so important to God's specific vision for your church?

Application Activity

Church History

• Who in the room has been in the church the longest?

• What were the most exciting times in the church's life?

• What was the vision of the church during those times?

Praying through the Vision

Objective: *Vision is birthed not out of logic, but from the deep parts of one's spirit. This lesson will lead the group to listen to and to pray for the things that stir our souls and trouble us about our world.*

Discovery Activity

What Bothers You?

- What are some things that "stir you up" at a heart level?

- What deeply held convictions do you have about ministry that might be a key to God's vision for your life?

- What needs do you see in your community that are not currently being met with which your church might be able to assist?

Learning Activity

Responding to Reality

When I heard these things, I sat down and wept. For some days I mourned and fasted and prayed before the God of heaven. Then I said: "LORD, the God of heaven, the great and awesome God, who keeps his covenant of love with those who love him and keep his commandments, let your ear be attentive and your eyes open to hear the prayer your servant is praying before you day and night for your servants, the people of Israel. I confess the sins we Israelites, including myself and my father's family, have committed against you. We have acted very wickedly toward you. We have not obeyed the commands, decrees and laws you gave your servant Moses.

"Remember the instruction you gave your servant Moses, saying, 'If you are unfaithful, I will scatter you among the nations, but if you return to me and obey my commands, then even if your exiled people are at the farthest horizon, I will gather them from there and bring them to the place I have chosen as a dwelling for my Name.'

"They are your servants and your people, whom you redeemed by your great strength and your mighty hand. Lord, let your ear be attentive to the prayer of this your servant and to the prayer of your servants who delight in revering your

name. Give your servant success today by granting him favor in the presence of this man."
  I was cupbearer to the king. —Nehemiah 1:4-11

The vision of Nehemiah was initiated as he listened to and sought to understand the dire state of Jerusalem. Upon doing so, he was powerless to do anything about it. He had no formal position of leadership of the Jewish people. He had a job as the cupbearer to the king of a foreign country. He did not live in Jerusalem. Nor was anyone looking to him to do something about the problem. As Andy Stanley writes, "He was in the wrong place with the wrong job working for the wrong guy. And he had no way of changing any of that."[2] Nehemiah could have very easily said, "Why doesn't someone do something about that." Or he could have blamed people saying, "Oh the obedience of the people of Jerusalem." He could have just gone back to his work saying, "That's not my problem."

Most of the time when we see a need, we find ourselves in similar situations to Nehemiah. There are situations and problems that bother us to the core of our souls, but we are powerless to impact them. And often this causes us to turn to things like complaining, blaming, or even ignoring.

Nehemiah did the only thing that he could do: He "wept, fasted and he prayed." He let the stirring of his soul turn into the only action available to him, the only thing that he could control. When God reveals the reality of the needs around us, we will find ourselves in the same place.

Discussion Questions:
1. What reality did Nehemiah see?

2. Put yourself in the place of Nehemiah. If you were he, how would you feel?

3. In the box below, identify the specific parts of his prayer.

Part 1	
Part 2	
Part 3	
Part 4	
Part 5	
Part 6	

Vision is the Priority for the Church

Every church has a vision, but not every vision is compelling or even positive. When interviewing leaders and focus groups about where they would like to see the congregation in the next three to five years, their answers focus on things like "full pews" and "full offering plates." This is more of a wish for institutional survival than a vision, especially when we consider the fact that we live in a world where attracting people to worship services is an increasingly ineffective way of reaching lost people with the Gospel.

Without an intentional vision of where a congregation is headed, a default vision will run in the background, thereby controlling decisions and actions. Most of the time, this default vision focuses on extending the past into the future. It focuses the congregation on where it has been more than on what God wants it to do to address needs.

When a church is young and new, vision is a priority because there is little history to extend into the future. In the early days of a church, vision is not only a necessity. It is the only option for survival. But this changes as a church develops over time.

When a church moves into a time of stability and starts maintaining, they are tempted to have a default vision of not rocking the boat too much. More of the same is the way to move into the future.

When a congregation is declining, they are tempted to focus on surviving, and they often do this by trying to recover the success of the past. For many declining congregations, the default vision is all about holding onto the Sunday services as long as possible.

The differences between a vision when a church is young verses when a church is maintaining or in decline can be explained when we understand the life cycle of a church. Like humans, churches progress through predictable life stages. Early in the life of the church, the birth, growth, and maturity are characterized by vision, action, and progress. But then the church becomes stable and moves into a state of maintaining the status quo. This naturally leads into a declining situation and if no changes occur death is the natural result.

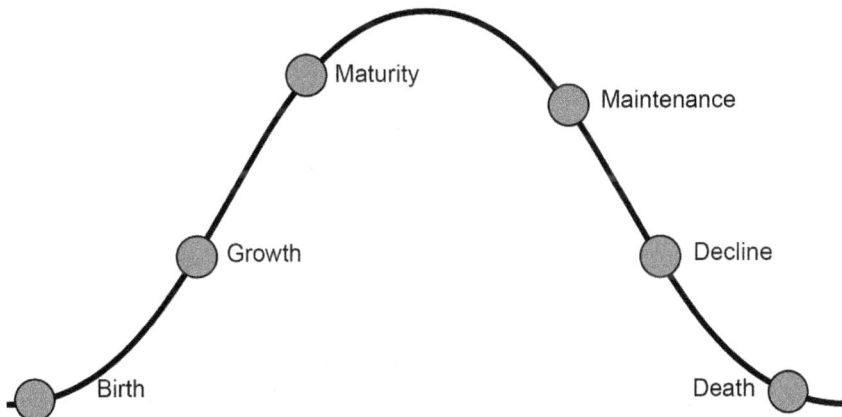

For many, the reality of the current life cycle stage of their church can be hard to swallow. Most of the time we don't look at reality with this kind of honesty. We tend to ignore the situation instead of dealing with it. The good news is that God is still at work in his church, and he does not see the death of any church as a good thing. This is why vision is so central to every church's future. Vision is the key that launches churches into new life cycles, but that is the point of the next lesson.

Discussion Questions:
• As you read through the paragraphs above, what stood out to you?

• What stage of the life cycle do you think your church is in?

• In your opinion, how might praying like Nehemiah promote the development of clear vision as a church?

Application Activity

Praying for the Vision of the Church

Spend time praying through the parts of Nehemiah's prayer. While there are a variety of ways to divide it up, the following four parts offer a simple guide for the time of praying together.

Worship:
Invocation for the Lord to See the Situation:
Confession of Corporate Failure to Live Up to God's Calling:
Petition for God to Act:

Faith and Vision

Objective: *Stepping out into new vision requires faith. When we walk in faith, the church will launch forth in new life. Through this lesson, the group will discover how vision and faith depend on one another.*

Discovery Activity

Describe and Draw

Share the results of your activity with the rest of the group.

1. What was it like to be the one trying to describe the picture?

2. What was it like to trust what you were hearing and translate it onto paper?

3. What was required for this activity to work?

Learning Activity

Vision Requires Faith

In the month of Nisan in the twentieth year of King Artaxerxes, when wine was brought for him, I took the wine and gave it to the king. I had not been sad in his presence before, so the king asked me, "Why does your face look so sad when you are not ill? This can be nothing but sadness of heart."

I was very much afraid, but I said to the king, "May the king live forever! Why should my face not look sad when the city where my ancestors are buried lies in ruins, and its gates have been destroyed by fire?"
The king said to me, "What is it you want?"

Then I prayed to the God of heaven, and I answered the king, "If it pleases the king and if your servant has found favor in his sight, let him send me to the city in Judah where my ancestors are buried so that I can rebuild it."

Then the king, with the queen sitting beside him, asked me, "How long will your journey take, and when will you get back?" It pleased the king to send me; so I set a time.

I also said to him, "If it pleases the king, may I have letters to the governors of Trans-Euphrates, so that they will provide me safe-conduct until I arrive in Judah? And may I have a letter to Asaph, keeper of the royal park, so he will give me timber to make beams for the gates of the citadel by the temple and for the city wall and for the residence I will occupy?" And because the gracious hand of my God was on me, the king granted my requests. So I went to the governors of Trans-Euphrates and gave them the king's letters. The king had also sent army officers and cavalry with me. —Nehemiah 2:1-9

A vision for the status quo does not require faith because you only have to look at what has worked in the past or at what is working now, and then try to reproduce it. New vision always requires faith because it requires that we trust God for something that we don't fully understand.

In order for Nehemiah to respond to the situation in Jerusalem, he had to have faith. He had to choose to step out into the unknown. He had to venture out of his comfort zone and trust God in ways that he had not done before.

The vision of God rides the back of faith. The Bible is full of people who advanced God's causes through faith. Hebrews chapter 11 is called the Hall of Faith, as it lists the Old Testament heroes who ventured on unknown paths to follow God while trusting his promises. The writer of Hebrews defines faith this way, "Now faith is confidence in what we hope for and assurance about what we do not see" (Hebrews 11:1).

In the space below, list the specific ways that Nehemiah demonstrated faith in the passage above.

Discussion Questions:
• In what ways did Nehemiah demonstrate faith in the passage above?

• If Nehemiah had lacked faith, what would have happened to the vision?

• How does faith involve risk?

• What role did planning play in the above story?

• Why is planning important to the fulfillment of vision?

Faith and Church Vision

In the previous lesson, we discussed how churches go through life cycles. In the early stages, vision is front and center. Vision was the driving force that gave focus to the values, the character, and the activities of a congregation. Amongst the complexity of a church organization composed of many different people doing all kinds of different things, vision during the early stages of the life cycle is the one overarching direction upon which everyone agreed.

But over time, this often changes. The vision becomes unclear in the midst of all the activities. The church begins to focus on doing lots of activities for the sake of doing those activities. Sometimes, those activities even compete or work against one another.

Life cycles are part of the normal development of an organization. There is no way to stop the process. We cannot go back to a previous stage or stop the process. The only way to move forward effectively as a church is to start a new life cycle.

And the only way to start a new life cycle is to catch a new vision, as illustrated by the diagram on the next page.

Starting a new life cycle will always require faith because your church has never done it that way before. God's vision for tomorrow is not simply an extension of the past. And for many this will be a huge test of their faith. But when we embrace the vision by faith, four things will occur as a result:

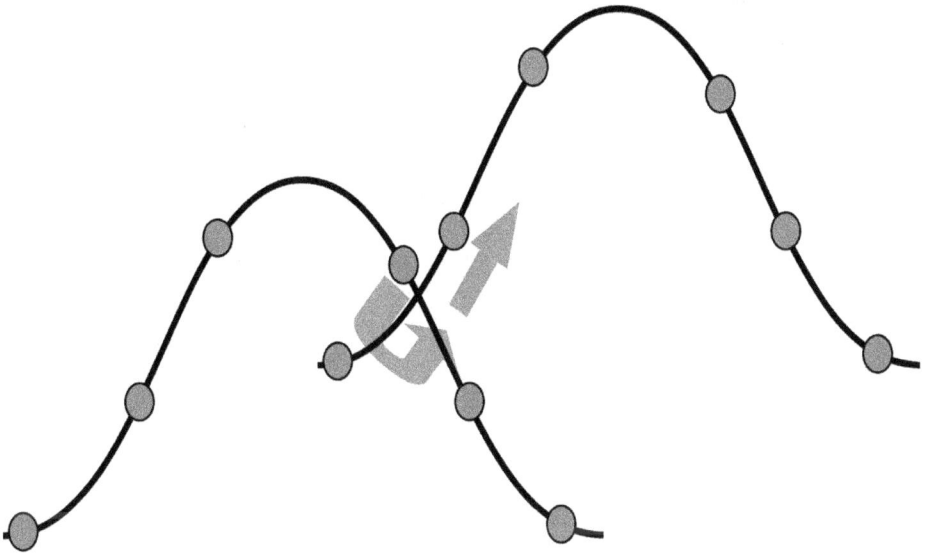

1. Passion—Vision stirs the heart and produces emotion. It moves beyond logic because they cast a vision for an anticipated future.
2. Motivation—Vision generates the ability to press forward and
   through struggles that would stand in the way.
3. Direction—Vision sets a course that helps to make decisions regarding what gets a "yes" and what gets a "no."
4. Purpose—Vision gives a person focus and a reason to move toward
   something significant. Without vision, a person does not know what
   to contribute. With it, even the small stuff matters.[3]

Discussion Questions:
• Why are these four things crucial to the life of a church?

• What happens when they are not present?

Application Activity

Think of a time in your life when you had a clear vision for something. Maybe it was related to your job, school, or in your personal life. It could be something like saving up for your education or working toward a promotion. How did that vision impact these four things?

What was the vision?

1. Passion

2. Motivation

3. Direction

4. Purpose

Articulation and Action

Objective: *Vision must be spoken and lived in order to come to life. In these conversations, the group will see how to talk about vision in a way that leads to action.*

Discovery Activity

How Does Vision Impact You?

In the previous lesson, we discussed how vision results in:

1. Passion—Vision stirs the heart and produces emotion. It moves beyond logic because they cast a vision for an anticipated future.
2. Motivation—Vision generates the ability to press forward and through struggles that would stand in the way.
3. Direction—Vision sets a course that helps to make decisions regarding what gets a "yes" and what gets a "no."
4. Purpose—Vision gives a person focus and a reason to move toward something significant. Without vision, a person does not know what to contribute. With it, even the small stuff matters.

Of these four, which do you feel is the most important? Why?

Learning Activity

Speak the Vision

I went to Jerusalem, and after staying there three days I set out during the night with a few others. I had not told anyone what my God had put in my heart to do for Jerusalem. There were no mounts with me except the one I was riding on.

By night I went out through the Valley Gate toward the Jackal Well and the Dung Gate, examining the walls of Jerusalem, which had been broken down, and its gates, which had been destroyed by fire. Then I moved on toward the Fountain Gate and the King's Pool, but there was not enough room for my mount to get through; so I went up the valley by night, examining the wall. Finally, I turned back and reentered through the Valley Gate. The officials did not know where I had gone or what I was doing, because as yet I had said nothing to the Jews or the priests or nobles or officials or any others who would be doing the work.

Then I said to them, "You see the trouble we are in: Jerusalem lies in ruins,

*and its gates have been burned with fire. Come, let us rebuild the wall of
Jerusalem, and we will no longer be in disgrace." I also told them about the
gracious hand of my God on me and what the king had said to me.
    They replied, "Let us start rebuilding." So they began this good work.*
                                            —Nehemiah 2:11-18

In order for vision to result in these four things listed in the Discovery
Activity, it is crucial for it to be clear. People have to understand the
vision. It cannot be hidden away in a strategy document for only key
leaders. It must be in front of the people on a regular basis.

This communication of vision works best when the following components
are included:

1. The issue that must be addressed
2. The way to address it
3. The reason that it must be done
4. Why it must be done now[4]

These four components are included in the story of Nehemiah above.
Take some time to read through the story again and identify them,
writing them in the table below.

The issue that must be addressed:
The way to address it:
The reason it must be done:
Why it must be done now:

Discussion Questions:
• What stands out to you from the reading in Nehemiah?

• What role did investigation play?

• How does vision relate to action?

Vision Words and the Church

The vision statement puts into words a picture of a preferred future. Think of it this way: If we took a snap-shot of a congregation 3-5 years from now, what would it look like? What things would be taking place that are not happening now? Like a photograph, the vision statement will include all kinds of details as well as giving an overall impression of what the congregation will look like. Not a picture of lots of smiling faces attending church services, but a picture of members serving in the community, interfacing with new people, sharing the Gospel while they share themselves with those around them. What places in the community would be in that picture? What demographic groups would be there? What kinds of specific needs would be met? There can be some goals and strategies included in the vision, but most significantly, we could see what we would look like accomplishing those goals and what the impact of our vision would look like for the people of our community.

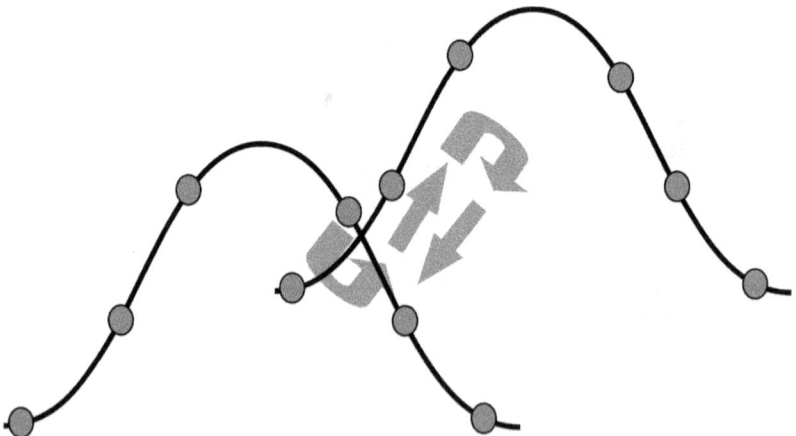

Vision statements are about vision clarity. Without clarity, a new life cycle might begin because people see the need for it initially, but it will be easy, too easy, to revert back to old patterns, and thereby reverting back to the default vision.

Effective church vision statements usually includes the following:

- An opening statement describing your mission target.
- A statement describing what compels you to reach out to this mission target.
- One or more statements that describe general strategy.
- One or more statements that describe a plan for reaching the mission target.

Here is an example from one church:

We are a church that is fully committed to meeting the needs of kids and their families. Jesus said, "Let the little children come to me, and do not hinder them, for the kingdom of heaven belongs to such as these"(Matt. 19:14). Our core value is children, and we seek to reach our community through an on-site sports ministry which includes soccer, basketball, and softball seasons. We dream in the next five years of building an all-purpose sports complex that will allow us to expand our Just 4 Kids sports ministry. This is broken down into three parts:

Vision Statement	Statement Id.
We are a church that is fully committed to meeting the needs of kids and their families.	Mission Target
Jesus said, "Let the little children come to me, and do not hinder them, for the kingdom of heaven belongs to such as these."	Mission Purpose
Our core value is children, and we seek to reach our community through an on-site sports ministry which includes soccer, basketball, and softball seasons.	Mission Strategy
We dream in the next five years of building an all-purpose sports complex that will allow us to expand our Just 4 Kids sports ministry.	Mission Plan

Discussion Questions:

• As a member of this church, why is it important for you to have the vision of the church very clear in your mind?

• What do you think would be the impact of such a clear understanding of the vision, if the majority of the church buys into it?

• How might such a clear vision change the way we do some things as a church?

• How might such a vision have an impact upon our community?

Application Activity

As you consider your commitment to the vision of your church, what do you need in order to be more fully invested in it?

❑ More information about the vision itself.
❑ More understanding of vision from a biblical point of view.
❑ More conversations about the practical implications of the vision.
❑ More exposure to the needs of the community so that you can understand God's vision for the people in your local environment.
❑ More time to think and pray about it.
❑ Other? _____

Are there things that might hinder you from being fully invested in the vision? Some might include:
❑ Too busy
❑ Fear of commitment
❑ Bad experience with a previous church and its vision
❑ Other? _____

When Opposition Comes

Objective: *Great vision is always met with opposition. This is just reality. How you deal with opposition is the question. The exercises in this session will prepare you to press on in the vision when it comes.*

Discovery Activity

Charades

Debrief
- What was your experience of the game?

- Did you notice something different about the game?

- Was there anything that was a distraction to your team?

- How was your vision for how the game was supposed to work opposed?

Learning Activity

When, Not If, Opposition Occurs

When Sanballat heard that we were rebuilding the wall, he became angry and was greatly incensed. He ridiculed the Jews, and in the presence of his associates and the army of Samaria, he said, "What are those feeble Jews doing? Will they restore their wall? Will they offer sacrifices? Will they finish in a day? Can they bring the stones back to life from those heaps of rubble—burned as they are?"

Tobiah the Ammonite, who was at his side, said, "What they are building— even a fox climbing up on it would break down their wall of stones!"

Hear us, our God, for we are despised. Turn their insults back on their own heads. Give them over as plunder in a land of captivity. Do not cover up their guilt or blot out their sins from your sight, for they have thrown insults in the face of the builders.

So we rebuilt the wall till all of it reached half its height, for the people worked with all their heart.

But when Sanballat, Tobiah, the Arabs, the Ammonites and the people of Ashdod heard that the repairs to Jerusalem's walls had gone ahead and that the gaps were being closed, they were very angry. They all plotted together to come and fight against Jerusalem and stir up trouble against it. But we prayed to our God and posted a guard day and night to meet this threat.

Meanwhile, the people in Judah said, "The strength of the laborers is giving out, and there is so much rubble that we cannot rebuild the wall."

Also our enemies said, "Before they know it or see us, we will be right there among them and will kill them and put an end to the work."

Then the Jews who lived near them came and told us ten times over, "Wherever you turn, they will attack us." —Nehemiah 4:1-12

In reflection on this passage, Andy Stanley writes about how vision naturally attracts opposition. He claims:

- Visions are easy to criticize.
- Visions attract criticism.
- Visions are difficult to defend against criticism.
- Visions often die at the hands of the critics.

He then goes on to identify two things that make a vision an easy target. He calls them:

CHANGE: Whenever you attempt to bring about change, it plays on the insecurities of those who have grown accustomed to the way things are and have always been. In this way, a vision is often seen as a threat. Consequently, it is not uncommon for the negative emotions a vision stirs up in people to be unleashed in the form of criticism. What you are convinced "should be" will be perceived by others as the very thing that "should not be." To make matters worse, the critics appear to be armed with the "facts." Often they have history and experience on their side. And understandably so. A vision is about the future, not the past. A vision has no history. And yet history and experience are what give birth to a vision. It is past experience that makes the visionary discontent with the way things are. It is from an understanding of history that a picture of what could be and should be takes shape. It is unfortunate that the fertile soil of history and experience is the very soil often used to bury a vision. The birthplace of a vision can become its burial ground as well.

GAPS: Visions are easy to criticize because of their inherent gaps. The very nature of a vision is that there is far more solid information on the what side of the equation than on the how side. There are holes in the plan. As long as someone simply wants clarification on what you want to see happen, you are in good shape. But once he begins questioning how you plan to pull it off, things get a little thin. But again, that is the nature of a vision. At least initially.

These gaps in the plan make visions easy targets for criticism. Ask enough "But what about …?" questions and you can dismantle just about any vision. The newer the vision, the more susceptible it is to the damaging, discouraging effects of this line of questioning. It is important to remember that it is the nature of a vision to have gaps. If there were no gaps, somebody else would have already delivered the goods. For this reason, every successful inventor, leader, and explorer faces criticism. You are in good company.[5]

Discussion Questions:
• Look back at the story regarding the opposition that Nehemiah faced. How did the fear of change promote opposition?

• How did gaps in the plan help make Nehemiah's vision an easy target?

• How have you experienced the fear of change when it comes to new ideas?

• How have you seen gaps in the plan derail good vision in the past?

Church and Vision Opposition

Vision is a clear picture of why a congregation exists. However, God's vision for a specific congregation often comes into competition with the vision of the institution of the church. While God sees the church growing because people find life in Him through Jesus, often the need to maintain the status quo of the organization causes people to resist anything that they do not understand. In fact, often people support a vision when it is new and exciting, but then once they start to see what the new vision really means, they resist it.

Some resist overtly. They fight against it. They complain about it. They blame the pastor for coming up with new ideas.

Others do so passively. They say that they are supportive of the leadership and the new vision, but their actions subversively undermine it.

When vision gives way to opposition, the generation of new life cycle for a church might begin, but its impact will be greatly diminished. The vision will wane and peter out. It might bring some change and new life, but it will fall far short of the impact that could have resulted. It might be illustrated in this way.

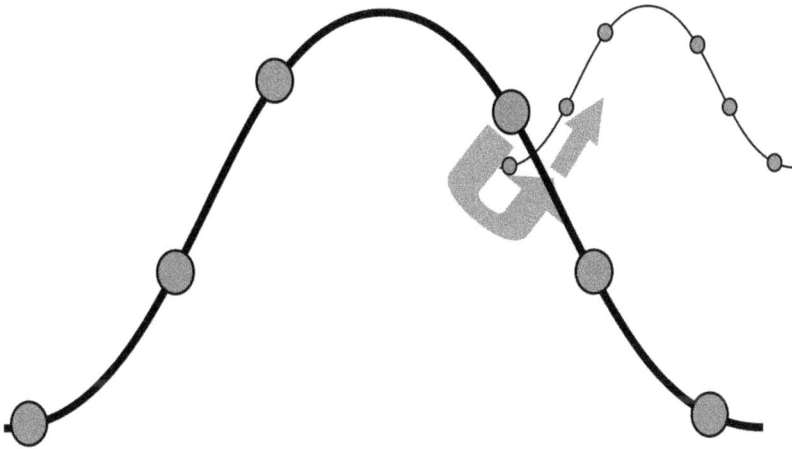

One of the reasons for opposition is that vision has an impact upon values and choices. When God reveals his specific vision, then it is the job of leaders to say yes to the things that line up with the vision and to say "no" to those things that don't. This will mean that many "good" projects or ideas will not line up with the vision. This is the reason that planning is so important when it comes to clear vision. If there is no plan for how the vision will be carried out, almost every idea that comes along will seem like a good idea.

Making these choices can be difficult and challenging. And almost always it involves a degree of risk. It will require saying no to things that don't line up with the vision and yes to things that will invite us our of our comfort zone.

Discussion Questions:
• How does fear of change effect you when it comes to new ideas?

• How do vision gaps impact your ability to move forward with new vision?

Application Activity

When you see a new idea and you feel resistance to it, what has been your typical response in the past? Take some time to fill out the following chart. Most people have responded in all of these ways to new vision. Think about church, work, or other situations where you have struggled with new ideas. How did you respond? What would you do differently next time?

Talk with Leadership	Passive Resistance	Overt Resistance	Typical Response
			Situation
			Your Response
			What Can You Learn

Vision and Unexpected Opportunities

Objective: *Clear vision will open doors to exciting, unexpected, and unpredictable opportunities, which in turn makes room for God to expand our vision. This session will prepare us to be watchful for the unexpected that can advance the vision.*

Discovery Activity

Church Dreams

- After working through this material about vision, what are your dreams for the church?

- How are these dreams different than they were before this study?

Learning Activity

Vision and Justice

Now the men and their wives raised a great outcry against their fellow Jews. Some were saying, "We and our sons and daughters are numerous; in order for us to eat and stay alive, we must get grain."

Others were saying, "We are mortgaging our fields, our vineyards and our homes to get grain during the famine."

Still others were saying, "We have had to borrow money to pay the king's tax on our fields and vineyards. Although we are of the same flesh and blood as our fellow Jews and though our children are as good as theirs, yet we have to subject our sons and daughters to slavery. Some of our daughters have already been enslaved, but we are powerless, because our fields and our vineyards belong to others."

When I heard their outcry and these charges, I was very angry. I pondered them in my mind and then accused the nobles and officials. I told them, "You are charging your own people interest!" So I called together a large meeting to deal with them and said: "As far as possible, we have bought back our fellow Jews who were sold to the Gentiles. Now you are selling your own people, only for them to be sold back to us!" They kept quiet, because they could find nothing to say.

So I continued, "What you are doing is not right. Shouldn't you walk in the fear of our God to avoid the reproach of our Gentile enemies? I and my brothers and my men are also lending the people money and grain. But let us stop charging interest! Give back to them immediately their fields, vineyards, olive groves and houses, and also the interest you are charging them—one percent of the money, grain, new wine and olive oil."

"We will give it back," they said. "And we will not demand anything more from them. We will do as you say."

Then I summoned the priests and made the nobles and officials take an oath to do what they had promised. I also shook out the folds of my robe and said, "In this way may God shake out of their house and possessions anyone who does not keep this promise. So may such a person be shaken out and emptied!"

At this the whole assembly said, "Amen," and praised the LORD. And the people did as they had promised.

Moreover, from the twentieth year of King Artaxerxes, when I was appointed to be their governor in the land of Judah, until his thirty-second year — twelve years — neither I nor my brothers ate the food allotted to the governor. But the earlier governors — those preceding me — placed a heavy burden on the people and took forty shekels of silver from them in addition to food and wine. Their assistants also lorded it over the people. But out of reverence for God I did not act like that. Instead, I devoted myself to the work on this wall. All my men were assembled there for the work; we did not acquire any land.

Furthermore, a hundred and fifty Jews and officials ate at my table, as well as those who came to us from the surrounding nations. Each day one ox, six choice sheep and some poultry were prepared for me, and every ten days an abundant supply of wine of all kinds. In spite of all this, I never demanded the food allotted to the governor, because the demands were heavy on these people.

—Nehemiah 5:1-18

God's vision is never about programs or projects. It's not about buildings or budgets. It's always about people. The rebuilding of the wall may have been Nehemiah's concrete vision, but the real vision was about meeting the needs of the people.

If we miss this, we miss what God is doing. And thereby we miss God's presence in the world because the projects we are doing for God get in the way.

This is why it is crucial that we keep our eyes open for unexpected opportunities to be God's hands and feet in the world. Nehemiah did this very thing. He had a vision to build a wall, but found that God also wanted to meet the needs of the people. He listened to the needs of the people and realized that they were being treated unjustly. Their basic necessities were not being met.

As governor, he had the right to a huge food allowance or stipend from tax money, however, he refused to take advantage of this position. By comparison, the daily food allotment for feeding 150 people was very modest when compared to other governing officials of the time. Nehemiah went beyond having a vision to accomplish a task. He had a vision for the people and thereby entered into the life with the people. He was called to rebuild the wall, but even more so, he was called to restore justice and wholeness to the people of God.

Discussion Questions:
• How did the lack of vision dishonor the poor and the outcast? How did it create selfishness and injustice?

• What did Nehemiah do to address the problem?

• How did a clear vision for building the wall create opportunities for touching lives of those who had been treated unjustly?

Church and the Unexpected

The most exciting part about the experience will be the unexpected ups and downs that are a part of the journey. No matter how much planning goes into it, no matter how much research is done, there will be serendipities along the way that will make it great. This is the way great ventures work. Life after all is lived in the moments, not in the planning.

Proverbs 16:9 tells us, "In their hearts humans plan their course, but the Lord establishes their steps." Planning is crucial, but the key is to walk in the moment and walk with God as you face the unexpected. Therein is the joy, the presence of God meeting us on the journey as we seek to walk in God's vision.

New vision launches us into a new life cycle as a church. Along the way of this new life cycle, like Nehemiah, we will encounter new opportunities and challenges that we did not expect. These unexpected opportunities create space to turn vision into new life. These opportunities propel us into the reality of the new vision, into the realization and fulfillment of that vision. And as a result, they have the potential to extend the new life cycle or even launch new ones.

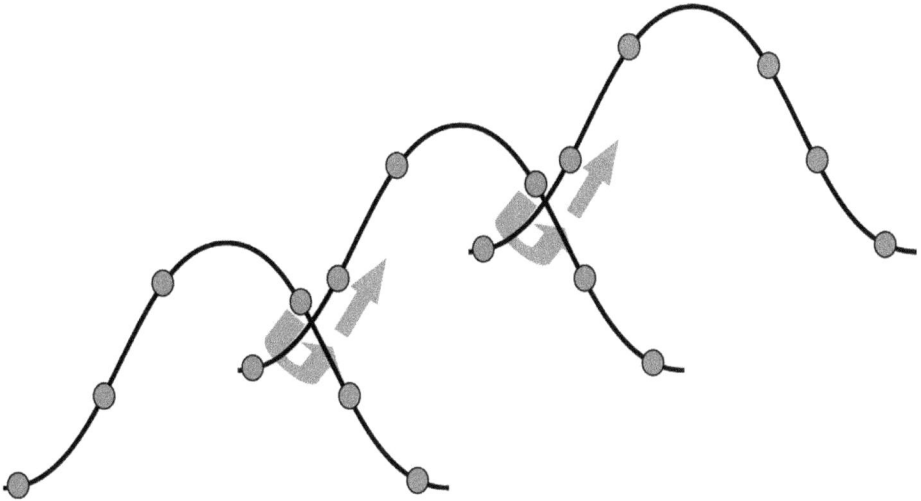

Discussion Questions:

• How has this study over the last six sessions been different than you expected?

• How have you seen God working in your life over the last few weeks that are different than you expected?

Application Activity

An Unexpected Journey

Close your eyes and take a deep breath. This is a time to reflect back over the last few weeks. God has been at work. Ask the Spirit of God to enliven your mind and heart to see what God has been doing. Read the questions below one at a time and then take time to reflect before moving to the next one. Write down whatever arises. Don't rush yourself. Just allow thoughts and ideas to come to mind.

• In what ways and places do you notice God having answered prayer?

• When has God's presence become real to you in unexpected times?

• How has God provided care for you?

• How has God cared for another through you?

• What bothers you when you reflect over the past few weeks?

• Where have there been struggles?

• What has energized you?

• What circumstances have depleted your energy?

Quietly sit with your responses and listen to what the Spirit of God might say to you in this moment.

Notes

[1] Andy Stanley, *Visioneering: God's Blueprint for Developing and Maintaining Personal Vision* (Colorado Springs: Multnomah, 2012), p. 17.

[2] Ibid., p. 30.

[3] Ibid., p. 8-12.

[4] Adapted from Ibid., p. 86.

[5] Ibid., p. 141-142.

www.ingramcontent.com/pod-product-compliance
Lightning Source LLC
Chambersburg PA
CBHW071651040426
42452CB00009B/1837